We call her

KILI

To Nancy,
always in prayer and sincerely

Dave Bartemes

Dave Bartemes

authorHOUSE®

AuthorHouse™
1663 Liberty Drive
Bloomington, IN 47403
www.authorhouse.com
Phone: 1-800-839-8640

Published by AuthorHouse   06/08/2012

ISBN: 978-1-4772-0395-8 (sc)
ISBN: 978-1-4772-0394-1 (hc)
ISBN: 978-1-4772-0393-4 (e)

Library of Congress Control Number: 2012908494

Contents

INTRODUCTION

By Richard L. Deming, MD
Medical Director
Mercy Cancer Center
Des Moines, Iowa

As a cancer doctor, I am inspired each and every day by the grace, grit, determination and compassion of my patients. Even with that experience and perspective, I could not have predicted the magnitude of the inspiration I was about to witness as I travelled to Africa with 19 cancer survivors on a journey to the summit of Mount Kilimanjaro. **Above + Beyond Cancer,** is a non-profit organization that I founded last year after we returned from a journey to Nepal. I had taken a group of survivors to Mount Everest Basecamp in April 2011 where we met up with adventurer Charlie Wittmack as he completed his World Triathlon by summiting Mount Everest. The success of the Everest Basecamp project was the catalyst that led to **Above + Beyond Cancer** and the Kilimanjaro climb in January 2012.

The survivors on our Kilimanjaro journey included 8 men and 11 women, ages 29 to 73, who had been treated for breast cancer, prostate cancer, thyroid cancer, salivary gland cancer, lymphoma, and leukemia. Some had been cancer-free for several years; some were still actively undergoing treatment for incurable cancer. The survivors came from every walk of life and included a priest, a professional viola player, an army officer, a cage fighter, a student, a farmer's wife, and a deacon. These amazing individuals were not athletes or mountain climbers who just happened to have cancer. In fact, they had never even dreamed of climbing a mountain. They signed up for this journey **because** of their cancer. They joined this team as a result of the confidence and courage they had gained during their cancer journey. They were not certain that they would be able to climb Kilimanjaro, but they were certain that attempting to climb Kilimanjaro would change their lives forever.

Dave Bartemes is a remarkable man. He and I first met in 2006. Dave had been diagnosed with prostate cancer in 1988. He had undergone surgery as his initial treatment. For many years it appeared that the surgery had been successful in curing him of his cancer. However, in 2006 his PSA blood test indicated that his cancer had returned and he began another long climb in his cancer journey. Throughout all the twists and turns of this journey, Dave has viewed his life as something much bigger than cancer.

His kind, compassionate, and reflective nature has allowed him to realize that cancer can be a teacher. As Dave journeyed onto the slopes of Kilimanjaro with our group in January, we were blessed to learn from him many life lessons that continue to inspire and motivate us.

After climbing Mount Kilimanjaro with this incredible group of survivors, I can tell you with certainty: **No one really knows what he or she is capable of accomplishing in life.** By reaching for something that is beyond the grasp of what is knowingly attainable, one can get a glimpse of his or her tremendous potential. We owe it to ourselves and to everyone whose life has been cut short by cancer, to live our lives fully and authentically with gusto and with passion. Not a single minute of our lives should be left un-lived. As we live our lives with passion, we should also reach out to others with generosity and compassion. Climbing a mountain can change one's life. Sharing one's story can change the world.

Dr. Deming and guide Charlie

FOREWORD

Charlie Wittmack
Executive Director
Above & Beyond Cancer

WHEN I WAS younger I believed that expeditions were like other sports that I had participated in as a child. Like sport, I believed that the goal of any expedition would always be clear and easily distilled to a simple concept. I believed that a team, in order to best achieve the set goal, should be strategically composed of people with the right talents and skills. I believed that an expedition would begin, and that it would end. And most of all, I believed that fulfillment would come from the satisfaction that results from completing what you set out to achieve.

What I have learned over the course of the last twenty years of exploration and adventure is that expeditions are not like sport. They're more like life.

We embark with a destination in mind, but the colorful fantasy that caused us to set out often fades to a black and white reality. We encounter challenges that we didn't imagine—challenges that require creativity and strength to overcome—which we occasionally struggle to find. Our friends and teammates disappoint us and fail. Strangers miraculously appear to take their places and help us move forward. And just as any great expedition doesn't have a clear beginning, it also doesn't have an end. Like a tree that falls into a river and changes the path of the water, expeditions change the course of our lives, subtly and slowly creating canyons where there had only been rock. Then, when we reach our destination—if we reach our destination—we look back over the great expanse and find that it was the journey that mattered. It was the journey that changed us. Perhaps it was the journey that we sought.

People who aren't naturally inclined to seek out wild and untraveled places are often confused by those of us who are. They see the suffering and discomfort, the danger and uncertainty, and they are left bewildered, and at times they are even left offended. They can't understand why someone would go to such great lengths and endure so much suffering to achieve something that they perceive to have so little value.

Oh, but what they don't know!

We go to the field, not for what is there, but for what isn't. It's a painful process, leaving the familiar behind, but a necessary one. We say goodbye to our friends and families, homes and beds, kitchens and bathrooms, telephones and fax machines . . . As we travel, we strip away all that is not life, all that distracts us from life, until we reach that distant place where we find that we are alone with ourselves.

In that moment, as we sit in that sacred space, we see the world clearly. We understand, perhaps for the first time, the meaning and significance of all the things that we had left behind. We also see ourselves in a new light. We acknowledge our weaknesses and grow to understand our true strengths.

With this new understanding, we return home, blessed by the experience, and filled with gratitude, forgiveness, and compassion. We see our lives, and all that fills our lives, as the incredible gifts they are. Then, with this new sense of fulfillment and purpose, life begins again.

Editor's Note:

Charlie Wittmack is a World Triathlon champion. In 2010, Charlie swam the length of the River Themes, crossed the English Channel to France swimming a total of 227 miles. He then rode a bicycle to Katmandu where he began a trek to the top of Mount Everest. It was an 11 month, 10,000 mile swimming, biking and climbing marathon. So far as is known, he is the only person to accomplish this feat.

IMPULSE

IMPULSIVENESS IS A characteristic that I have in large measure. Over the years I have learned that acting on impulse can be good or bad, depending on the outcome. I once walked into the office of an architect who had been specifying a competitor's products for years, pulled out a chair, emptied my pockets; and then I stood on my head atop the chair. After about 10 seconds I righted myself and said, "Mr. Chambers, I'll stand on my head to get a contract on your next job." With that, I left his office. When I returned to my workplace there was a message from Mr. Chambers, "Meet with me and my associate tomorrow at 9:00, and we'll start on the specs for the East End Tower."

There's no question that my desperation impulse could have backfired. Mr. Chambers could just as well have called my boss and complained bitterly about my "unprofessional" behavior; in which case, I may well have been fired. Be that as it may, this story circulated in our home office until the day I retired.

And so it is with impulse. On a day in November, 2011, I read a story in the Des Moines Register about a group

1

of cancer survivors who had hiked to the base camp of Mount Everest. The article mentioned that there would be another trip, sponsored by *Above and Beyond Cancer*, an organization that promotes healthy living and physical activity for cancer survivors, and anyone else interested in healthy living practices. On impulse, I sent e-mails to Dr. Richard Deming, the author of the article and the founder of *Above and Beyond Cancer*, and Charlie Wittmack, the Executive Director. I received a response the next day telling me that the group was planning a trip to Africa, where we would climb to the highest point on that continent, Mount Kilimanjaro.

Two weeks later, while I was working on my farm gathering data on a stand of northern pecan, my cell phone rang interrupting a lengthy calculation. At first I didn't want to answer the phone, it was an intrusion into a pleasant day working with the District Forester and planning for the future: but on impulse, I answered the phone.

It was Dr. Deming. He called to tell me that I had been selected to be a participant on the trip to Tanzania, and Mount Kilimanjaro. I couldn't contain my excitement, so I immediately told the District Forester my good news. I called my wife to tell her. I left messages for my sons and their families. I was impulse driven; I told everyone I met over the next few days about the opportunity I had to experience a new adventure.

MARY

MY NEW ADVENTURE came with a realization that if I were going to climb a mountain in Tanzania, I'd better be well prepared. I had been working out at a gym near my home for over three years. I felt like I was in pretty good shape. In my youth, I had been active in sports and was a collegiate swimmer. Still, 73 years on this earth had taken its toll. Over the years I had had several surgeries, including a radical prostectomy for prostate cancer. I had also grown from my swimming weight of 155 to an almost obese, 218. Years of travel, good meals and good wine, had caught up with me. Something had to be done.

Part of the program for *Above and Beyond Cancer*, is the inclusion of good training and good diet practices. I had scheduled a meeting with a dietitian at the Mercy Cancer Center in Des Moines, and; the *Above and Beyond* trainer had contacted me for an appointment to discuss my training needs.

I met Mary at her home on a Saturday morning, the day after my meeting with the dietitian. Mary met me at the door with her two children, Anna, 11, and Luke, 10. I was comfortable immediately. Anna and Luke were well schooled in good manners and they were just as outgoing as their mother. Each extended his and her hands in greeting and welcomed me. The home was on a corner in a middle class neighborhood just west of downtown Des Moines. The neighborhood has many mature trees and is well kept. Mary told me that she and her husband, Matt, enjoyed the location because it was near to, and had a walking connection with, Water Works Park; an ideal place to run, hike, and view the trees in the arboretum.

After the kids went off to play, Mary and I sat at the kitchen table to discuss my training program. To my surprise, what Mary was telling me about exercise and diet was a repeat of what the dietitian told me the day before. Our conversation ranged over a number of subjects including education, growing up, and religion. I couldn't help noticing that the house was well kept and neat. The only exception was that there were a few misplaced cushions and a dropped shirt or pajama top by the stairs; clear evidence of the presence of active children. After our discussion, we set a time to meet at the Healthy Living Center in Clive. I left knowing that we were both using the same playbook.

Once at the Healthy Living Center, Mary continued the good impressions of our first meeting. She is an attractive 40 year old who has been training for years. She smiles and laughs easily as she dances through the routines. She would often wear a red ball cap and let her long black ponytail stream out the back. She is so light on her feet that I was intimidated by my clumsiness; but she stuck with me, always paying attention to technique, and always encouraging me to do just a bit better. "Good job;" "turn it up;" "one more time," she would repeat often and loud. I learned right away that working out with someone else is a lot more fun than being by myself. On more than one occasion she would reach to the stair stepper panel and punch the degree of difficulty up. The other thing I learned was that exercise, when one must work out alone, is a good time for thinking and listening to your own heartbeat.

In addition to the personal training, Mary conducted group training one evening each week. It was during these group sessions that I realized how poorly I was doing. I was always last as the group moved along the running track, first jogging, then high knee lifts, then ankle kicks, followed by crossovers, and so on, around and around the track. Mary and the others would skip to a rapid pace and I would lag behind huffing and puffing like a steam engine. It wasn't going well, but I continued to train daily as I was determined that I would make it to the top of Kilimanjaro. "I may get there last," I would tell everyone, "but I will finish!"

I became frustrated with my progress, but Mary would continue to encourage me. During our workouts we would talk about family, friends, work, whatever came to mind. Over the course of two months I began to appreciate Mary's dedication and expertise. But there was something else about Mary. Her personality was winsome. She could keep the chatter going when everyone else was sucking air.

One evening she told us that if she "lapped" us when we were running on the track, she would "swat you on the butt as I go by." Her playfulness was part of every workout. She always had a smile, but the smile was always buttressed with sincerity and professionalism. When the group sessions began, we were all looking to Mary as leader, mentor, and friend. Mary is well loved and she loves well.

There was just one thing about working out at the Healthy Living Center in Clive instead of my usual gym in Urbandale. That was, the gym in Clive was several miles away instead of practically in my backyard, so I would change and shower at the gym instead of just hurrying home in my gym clothes. At first I didn't realize what difference this would make, but it did make a difference. I noticed this change when I went for my first workout at the Healthy Living Center.

Mary Van Heukelem

THE LOCKER ROOM

I KNOW ABOUT locker rooms. I spent a great deal of time in locker rooms during high school and college. Before and after practice, before and after games; the locker room was where all the players met to study the game plan. The locker room was where we dressed and showered. Locker rooms are damp, wet, and smell like sweat. Locker rooms echo as doors open and close. Sometimes locker rooms are loud with voices shouting over one another, and sometimes they are so quiet that you can hear a shower dripping. Locker rooms today are cleaner, larger, and better equipped than the locker rooms of my youth, but the sounds, smells, and heavy air are the same.

If I know so much about locker rooms, and about the men who frequent them, then why did I hesitate before entering on that day this past November? It had been more than a quarter century since I gave up competitive swimming. The busyness of life had taken over; as a husband and father with an extended work week, I didn't have time for swimming. Besides, age was taking seconds off my times and the younger guys were better than ever.

Locker rooms of old were where men divided into groups or changed individually at their lockers. There are sometimes special sections in locker rooms for regular members or for teams. The locker room at my college had a swim team section that no one else dared to enter. If a team member failed to make the cut, or decided to quit, he was immediately ejected from the team section. One thing about locker rooms today that has remained the same, is that when you talk to another man in a locker room, you make sure that you are looking him in the eye.

But why hesitate? I know that men in locker rooms undress in plain view. I know that they walk to the showers naked as the day they were born; not nearly as pretty, but just as naked. I hesitate because I'm afraid they will know. I don't know how they will know, but somehow they will know. Someone may tell them that I'm part of a cancer group that's going to Kilimanjaro. Someone may notice that I slip a pad into my shorts while I'm dressing. I need the pad because I drip, and when I exert myself I spurt urine uncontrollably. They will figure it out; and they will know.

I was diagnosed with prostate cancer 23 years ago in December of 1988. The urologist at The Mayo Clinic in Rochester, Minnesota, praised my family physician for his skill at detecting a hard spot during a routine examination. He then explained that he believed surgery to be the best option. He went on to explain all the possible side effects of the surgery, including incontinence and impotence.

He explained the surgery itself, and then closed with a direct statement, saying; "If you don't have surgery soon, I believe you'll be dead in 5 years." I had surgery the next morning.

Once in the locker room I looked for an out of the way place where I could put on my workout clothes. In short order I found a changing room. It was also a changing room that hadn't been used for a while. Maintenance had yet to discover that the lights were all burned out, so I changed in the dark. That was OK by me because I didn't want anyone to know.

I didn't want anyone to know because the pad I use is a feminine pad. I researched the project well. At first I tried several of the pads in the male department; too big, too bulky, not practical at all. My wife suggested that I try a small feminine pad. "Good idea," I thought. So I slipped a package into the shopping cart; and let her check out.

The incontinence factor may seem like a small thing to some people. Some might think I should do what I need to do and get on with it. I wish it were that simple. Incontinence can attack at any moment. All it takes is a move in the wrong direction, or a beautiful woman walking past. Sometimes sitting for a long period of time causes backup, and when you stand up, the security of the "pad" is demolished. I've had to race home to change on many occasions.

While the incontinence factor weighs every day, it is overshadowed by the "impotence" factor. While it's hard enough to admit incontinence, its nigh on impossible to even mention impotence. I couldn't help noticeing that all of my physicians shy away from a discussion about impotence except in the purely technical terms of advising of the possibility. After surgery, after radiation, and after hormone treatment; the subject only comes up if I bring it up.

Every day I give thanks for the success of my surgery. Eight years ago I experienced a recurrence of cancer. This time the suggested treatment was radiation. Once again, the doctor told me about the possible side effects: more incontinence, and possibly impotence. The treatment was easy enough, painless, with no recovery as with surgery. Unfortunately, the treatment was effective for only a few months.

This time my cancer would be treated with a form of hormone therapy. There was no discussion about "possible" side effects. The doctor's statement was emphatic; I would almost certainly experience impotence.

Back in November, when I returned to the locker room after my workout that first day of training for the trek to the top of Kilimanjaro, I changed in the darkened changing room. I was sheepish about changing my clothes in front of others, and I was sheepish about using a changing room that no one else used. One way or another, I was out of step with other men who seemed oblivious to being naked in front of each other. After my workout, I went home to shower.

The next time I went to the Healthy Living Center for a workout, I determined that I wouldn't use the changing room. I put on my gym clothes facing my locker. I did the same when the workout was over. Over the next six weeks I became more comfortable in the locker room, even when men were changing next to me. I also became more at ease walking to the shower and drying off in front of my locker.

I don't know if I will ever be completely comfortable changing my clothes in front of other men. I do know that I will do my best to overcome the anxiety that I feel. I also know, in my rational mind, that none of the men care; or even think, about whether or not I'm incontinent or impotent. They are simply there to do what they came to do. It's up to me to do the same. The only difference is; now I understand a little bit more about locker rooms. I also understand a little bit more about me.

After my initial diagnosis, I was referred to a local urologist for further testing. His office was small, with only six or seven chairs and two dim lamps in the waiting room. The receptionist checked me in in a matter of fact way, with hardly a "hello" or "how are you" in speech or manner. There were four other men ahead of me so I settled down for what I thought would be a long wait. The other men sat in silence. One was reading a magazine and the other three were waiting with their arms folded. One by one they were called for their appointments.

When the nurse called my name, it was in the same manner in which I was received by the receptionist, very matter of fact, and without greeting or other communication except for a flat "How are you today?" She showed me into a waiting room where I found a chair and again wondered how long I would be waiting. Almost immediately, the doctor knocked on the door and entered.

He was an older man whose manner was identical to that of his office staff. His greeting was in a low voice and he used as few words as possible as he set about the business of a prostate exam. It wasn't long before I realized that it was his manner that had been adopted by everyone around him. It was assembly line medicine at its worst. "Drop your trousers, lean forward," he said in a monotone as he proceeded. He then said in the same voice, "Yes, there's a lump that needs to be checked out."

My own feelings at this point were that we were going through routine and boring motions. So far nothing in my life was changed or changing. "This will soon be over and I will go home for dinner and a good weekend," I thought. Then he said in that same monotone, "We'll have to take a sample and do a biopsy." He took an instrument out of a drawer that I couldn't see very well, and asked me to lean over the exam table, he inserted the instrument and then I heard a loud "snap" as he lanced my prostate gland.

Everything changed. My head began to swirl, dizziness welled over me, and my legs began to grow limp; the room darkened. I slowly slid to the floor into a state of semi consciousness. I couldn't control my arms or legs but I was aware that the doctor and his assisting nurse were now in rapid motion and giving each other commands. I lay on the cold floor with my trousers and shorts down by my ankles, unable to move. The doctor covered my nakedness and the nurse wet a towel and put it over my forehead and face. I gradually regained my strength, felt the cool towel, and then became more and more aware of my surroundings. I pulled my trousers up and sat on the floor for a while as the dizziness faded. The doctor helped me to my feet and I said nothing, embarrassed by what had happened.

When I got home that evening I told my wife about the exam, but nothing about my going into shock over such a minor procedure. My weekend was anything but normal. I spent time in front of the TV, but not watching or listening. I began to wonder if I might really have cancer. My thoughts wound around and around in my head, and for quite a while I prayed. I think that this was the first time in my life that I prayed with the connecting idea of mortality as part of my prayer. I was 50 years old.

My follow up appointment with the urologist was one week later, again on a Friday. When I entered the office there was no one in the waiting room. The receptionist was cheerful and greeted me with a happy, "How are you today, Mr. Bartemes?" The nurse came to the door of the waiting room almost immediately. She also asked how I was doing, and engaged in a bit of small talk as she showed me to the doctor's office. Her manner was deferential, and I realized that while this might have been routine, it was different. By the time I was seated in the office, I knew that I would be getting bad news.

To this day I don't remember which route I drove to get home that evening. I do remember that it had been a sunny day but by the time I left the office, evening was creeping in, and the sky was dull. When I arrived home Cora met me on the stairs. She was on the top step and I stopped one step below. Now, face to face, I told her that the biopsy was positive and that I would have to have either surgery or radiation. I also told her that I asked the doctor for a referral to the Mayo Clinic for a second opinion. We embraced for a long time in silence as I began to worry about her and the boys. I have always been a person who prayed. That weekend I prayed a lot.

Today I continue to go to the Healthy Living Center to work out. But there are differences. I notice that when I leave my car in the parking lot, my step quickens. I am eager to get to the door and to start my exercise program. When I enter I almost always see someone I recognize and I respond to their "Good morning" with my own. I keep my quick step as I go into the locker area; put my bag on a bench, and open one of the lockers.

The trek to Kilimanjaro was an "opening" for me. It gave me an opportunity to expand my horizons. The preparation was hard, but fun. The trip and the hike were hard, but fun. Writing my journal is hard, but fun. Now I go into the locker room to do what I came to do, just like everyone else. I change and shower, just as naked as everyone else. I stand in the bright lights and talk with others, just like everyone else. Outward, I might look and act just as the others, but there is a difference. It's a difference that is difficult to explain, but a difference nevertheless.

FAMILY

I WAS BORN and raised in West Virginia. My childhood was idyllic. I spent many happy days venturing into West Virginia's woods and waters. I had an older brother, younger sister, and many relatives nearby. We always had plenty of food and a roof over our heads, but there were times when money was scarce. By today's standards we would have been called poor, but we didn't know it. I was blessed to be educated by the Sisters of St. Francis of Stella Niagara, the Salesian priests and brothers of New Rochelle, and by the professors and instructors at West Virginia State College. My family was, and is, Catholic through and through.

West Virginia State College was more than a college to me. It was where I was transformed from a happy go lucky kid into a spirited adult who learned to speak up for justice and equality in a segregated world. It was where I bonded with friends of another race and culture, and participated in some of the sit-ins and picketing of the late 1950's. It was also where I met the love of my life, Cora.

Cora was a pretty girl who was also a straight "A" student. The family joke is that after we met my grades went up and hers went down. Nevertheless, she graduated Summa Cum Laude and was inducted into the honorary society, Alpha Kappa Mu; all this in spite of being visually impaired from birth. It was after we met that I was named to the All Scholastic Varsity. Cora was good for me from the start. We have been married for more than 51 years and we have three sons, all married, and nine grandchildren.

Cora is not only the love of my life; she has two qualities that have been influential in whatever successes I have managed. She is both my biggest cheerleader, and the one who slows me down so I don't react to my impulses too quickly or too strongly. She has always had the ability to present alternatives in a way that caused me to think of negative consequences. After I told her about the trip to Tanzania, and Mount Kilimanjaro; her immediate reaction was positive. After a few days, however, she began to ask the questions that needed to be asked. "How are you going to deal with the gastrointestinal problems that you have on a regular basis? It's going to be more physically demanding than anything you've done in years; are you sure you can do this?" We discussed the ordeal in detail, and I continued to insist that I wanted to go. She accepted my decision.

It wasn't just Cora that had to be sold on my trip to Kilimanjaro. The children and grandchildren had a say in this. Their initial reaction was one of disbelief, followed by a lot of questions. The most frequent question was: "Are you sure you want to do this?" The second most asked question was: "Why do you want to do this?" I didn't have any great earth-shaking answers except that "I'm going." Once this message got through their reaction was: "You go, G-dad." My grandchildren often refer to me as "Deacon G-Dad." Somehow or other the moniker has transferred to other kids their age and I heard many younger people in our congregation give me encouragement by saying "Go for it, G-dad."

DEPARTURE

GENERAL CONSENSUS ABOUT traveling is that airplanes are horrid. It's true. The hassle of air travel makes me dread going anywhere on an airplane. Unfortunately, it's the only practical way to get to Africa. There were, however, some good things to say about our flights to Kilimanjaro. We were reasonably on time, our connections were easy, and we were flying nearly the whole way in daylight. This wasn't true for two of our fellow travelers; Mike and Brandon missed their connection in Detroit, missed again in Amsterdam, and ended up getting to Kilimanjaro three days late.

The daylight leg of the trip from Amsterdam to Kilimanjaro was the best. We flew east toward Berlin, turned south to cross the Italian Alps; then down the Dalmatian Coast of the Adriatic and across the Mediterranean. We crossed into Egypt, and from 37,000 feet I could see the waters of Lake Nasser formed behind the Aswan Dam. The extent of the sand dunes of Western Egypt is incredible: I could see thousands of miles of desert with no sign of life, not even a road. Shadows from the setting sun played tricks on my eyes as we sped to Kilimanjaro. Shortly after sunset we landed at the Kilimanjaro Airport 30 hours after leaving Des Moines. All that time in the air helped me coalesce my thoughts about why I was taking on the challenge of climbing Kilimanjaro.

I wanted to learn more about Tanzania. I wanted to meet the people and to understand their culture and history. I wanted more than just an adventure up the mountain. That was important, but I wanted more. I wanted to get to know the other survivors and the caregivers who would be with me. Some I knew from our workouts, but there were new faces. I wanted to know where they were from, and why they wanted to climb Kilimanjaro. There is so much to learn and so much to do. I doubted if two weeks would be enough for me.

AFRICA

MY FIRST AIRPLANE flight was in 1961. It was a humdinger! I flew on a Military Air Transport Service DC 6 from Fort Gordon, Georgia, to Fort Dix, New Jersey. I don't remember the name of either airport, but I do remember that the airport in New Jersey looked an awful lot like the airport in Kilimanjaro where I landed on Monday, January 2, 2012. It was small, crowded, mostly open air, and without air-conditioning; the baggage conveyers were the only evidence that we were in the 21st century rather than the mid-20th.

The airport was a jumble of bodies searching for duffle bags. Since many of the faces were new to me, I had a lot of difficulty sorting out who was who. This has been one of my great failings in life. It takes me a while to put a name to a face and remember all the players on a team. This was a problem for me throughout the Kilimanjaro adventure and I still get some of the team mixed up. After about 40 minutes, our crew managed to be outside together, each person clutching or dragging his or her duffle bag. At this point the duffle was a better indicator of who was a part of our group than the names or faces.

Our busses were waiting for us, and the drivers and assistants got busy putting our duffels on top. The busses are more like oversize vans. Each one can carry about 20 passengers, provided the luggage is put on top of the bus. This is standard practice in Africa. We were told that our ride to our first hotel would take about 40 minutes so everyone settled down trying to make the best of a bumpy, swervey, uncomfortable ride.

Suddenly, someone shouted, "Look, Zebras!" We all craned our necks to look out a window to see their first African wildlife. The driver put the headlights on bright, and we could see two or three burros in the high beams crossing over the road: so much for African wildlife on our first day.

We arrived at the AMEG Lodge just after 9 p.m. Dinner was ready for us, and we were ready for dinner. At the time I didn't know it, but this was a portent of some bad things to come. It turned out that meal times in Tanzania, run very late into the evening. Breakfast is at a reasonable hour, 7:30-8:30; but lunch usually isn't served until 2:00 or 3:00 p.m. Dinner is put off until 9:00 p.m. or later. For me this is a disaster, as my gastrointestinal problems are exacerbated if I eat after 5:00 p. m

Kilimanjaro at sunrise from AMEG Lodge.

Day One

Our first full day in Moshe, a city of 2,200,000 people, and the largest city near Mount Kilimanjaro; would include a hike to nearby Marangu Falls. After a typical African breakfast of fresh pineapple, papaya, mango, eggs, bananas, potatoes, and a local pancake, we boarded the vans for a trip to the falls. The hike was a killer. The descent into the canyon was nearly vertical. Steps were cut into the side of the gorge by hand and by foot traffic. They were often 2-3 feet in height, and some rickety handrails were attached to trees and stakes. Sometimes the stakes were so wobbly that they were more dangerous than none at all.

We hiked around the canyon for several hours and went to the bottom last. There were a number of homes nearby and the people were always ready to greet us. Children in particular would run up to our path and answer our greeting with "Jumbo;" Swahili for "Hello." This greeting was universal throughout our trip and the people always responded with smiles. I felt comfortable with the people from day one.

Dave at Marangu Falls

The climb back to the top of the canyon was extremely difficult for me. I found my endurance to be short. One of the younger climbers helped by taking my back pack. By now all the others were aware that I struggled on the uphill. My upper body weight was too much for my legs. This was quite an embarrassment for a guy who, as a young man, relied on his legs to power through a 1500 meter swim in college, or run for touchdowns in high school. At this point I'm starting to realize that, no matter how I feel inside, or how much my mind is telling me that I could always do more; my legs would rebel and my lungs would gasp as a result of 73 years on this earth.

Lunch was at a local outdoor restaurant operated by a family. Fried chicken, potatoes (there were always potatoes) rice and some sauces. The fried chicken was good, the sauces not so good. I ate heartily at this lunch, thinking that I would go easy at dinner in order to protect myself from midnight miseries. This turned out to be a good plan as dinner wasn't until 9:00 p.m. Unfortunately, dinner consisted of the best fruit salad and best fish curry I've ever eaten. I ate only a little bit of each and weathered the night well.

Day Two

I awoke to the call to prayer by a local Mizzen. It was pleasant to hear the call and I drifted immediately into my own prayer. A local Chanticleer contributed his voice to the morning music and I prayed especially for my wife and family. I was peaceful for the next hour, even as I contemplated the difficulty of the day before; and what I might encounter in the days ahead.

The morning was bright and clear. The top of Kilimanjaro reflected ribbons of pink from the rising sun. The mountain is massive. It is difficult to realize that the peak, which looks so near to the Lodge, is really 40 miles away. The glaciers spill down the mountain in white streams and then disappear leaving bare rock for the eye.

Before breakfast many of us joined Tomoko for a half hour of yoga. We reached for the blue sky to stretch muscles before Kilimanjaro. We fell into ritual poses before that great mountain and the sinew of arms and legs flexed as if in genuflection to this wonder that God presented. The air felt soft, clean, fresh, and filled with promise. This day was sweeter than the fruit of breakfast. This day was overflowing with anticipation. This was our Advent before Christmas.

After breakfast we packed and waited for the high clearance busses that would take us to the entrance to Kilimanjaro National Park. By 10:00 a.m. the crew had loaded our duffle bags and we loaded ourselves onto the busses and began the 2 hour ride. Leaving Moshe, we passed patches of fertile ground. These were near streams and there were always people living in and around the plots of bananas, plantains, corn and other local crops. As the ground rose in elevation we entered an area of near desert. Here were small herds of cattle and goats shepherded by men, women, boys and girls. The land was nearly bare with only patches of grasses. Some of the herders, especially the goat herders, were no more than 10 or 11 years old.

Poverty stretched in every direction. Homes were usually small one or two room enclosures with dirt floors. The kitchen area was in front of the home where the women and girls prepared food over open fires. Women carried loads on their heads. These loads could be almost anything; fruit, firewood, or baskets filled to the brim with whatever needed to be moved from one place to another. Men would also serve as bearers of burden, but their wares were usually different. Men would carry the heavier items, planks, and cans of fuel, metal, or other items that wouldn't fit the classification of "domestic." Men would use bicycles, motorbikes, pull carts, and push carts of every description to move materials. Some few would be fortunate enough to have a car or pickup truck from which to conduct business.

These vehicles were a perfect fit for the word, "beater." In the 12 days I was in Africa, I didn't observe one woman driving a vehicle although our guides told us that women did drive.

After about two hours, the landscape changed again. We were now at about 4500 feet above sea level and in an area of more rainfall and cooler temperatures. As the dry area gave way to a moist zone, we began to see planted forests. The trees were invariably the tall, small diameter pines that are native to the area. They were planted in plots of about 10 acres each. The rows of trees were as straight as Iowa corn in August. One of the most interesting features of the planting was that in the newly planted stands, where trees were no more than 6-feet tall, they had interplanted potatoes. As we passed through the area we witnessed hundreds of men, women and children harvesting the potatoes by hand and shovel. There were thousands of tall white bags of potatoes by the roadside waiting to be loaded onto trucks. Each bag appeared to contain about two bushels. I learned later that the government of Tanzania has a large university sponsored tree research program, and that tree planting has a high priority throughout the country.

Forestry Plantation

Once we arrived at the entrance to the National Park, we had to wait several hours to register and gather our guides and porters for the trek. This is when I learned for the first time what is meant by the term "drop toilet." Once inside the small building where the toilet is located it all becomes clear. A drop toilet is nothing more than a hole in the floor. There's nothing to hold on to; nothing to offer any support of any kind, and no instructions are offered. All I will add to this is that they are inconsiderate of the elderly.

We passed the time until mid afternoon by playing word games. We formed a big circle for an hour or so of Charades. About 3:00p.m., we learned that the road to our trailhead had been washed out by a recent storm and that we would have to take an alternate route. Also, we were more than a half day behind schedule, so instead of hiking to our planned bivouac we would camp at the trailhead and begin our walking journey the next morning. With that we piled into the trucks and started for the trailhead.

We didn't go very far before we came to a narrow road that was pitted with ditches, washouts, and trees so close that they rubbed the side of the truck. The driver shifted into bulldog low to navigate the ditches, and the engines growled and strained as we crawled along dipping and swaying. We tossed back and forth in our seats and on several occasions I thought that we might actually tip over. After an hour we came to a washout that was too deep and dangerous for the trucks to pass. We would hike to the trailhead from this point.

The trail was relatively flat, but had a lot of water and mud. It was easy walking with only a few dodges and jumps to go around the mud. We got to the trailhead about 5:00 p.m. Some of the porters and guides were already there preparing dinner, and setting up tents.

THE GENERAL

DR. DEMING AND Charlie Wittmack called us together as soon as we arrived at the trailhead. Dr. Deming introduced us to our chief guide, a man who introduced himself as "Major General Chombo." One look at the man and I knew that this was a man who expected to be in charge. He stood about 5 feet 10 inches tall, but was about a yard wide at the shoulders. He appeared to be in his early thirties, but I suspect he was older. He spoke to us in good English and in a manner that convinced me that he was made of tough metal. General Chombo let us know in no uncertain terms that we would follow his lead in all matters related to the climb to Kilimanjaro. He then broke away from the group and began supervising the porters in their duties.

General Chombo was dressed in the attire of a trekker. His clothes fit loosely and his legs were large and supported the bulk of his body easily. He moved in a slow, deliberate manner with eyes that could take in the wide expanse of the trailhead. I wouldn't describe his eyes as "penetrating" but rather as "knowing." His face and hands were the dark chocolate brown of the local people and his complexion was clear, smooth, and unblemished. His demeanor and bearing spoke the truth that he was a "General."

Dr. Deming suggested that those who wanted to go on a one hour hike gather with him. It was just a way to get us out of the way so the porters could get the tents up and dinner on. I was all in for the hike as we had spent the whole day standing around and sitting in the trucks. I needed a workout.

The trail leading out of the camp was steep and slippery. It was so steep that the many thousands of hikers who had preceded us had kicked steps into the hillside. Many of the steps included stepping over rocks and roots at the same time. We hiked about a half mile before we got to a small space that was relatively flat. I was gasping for air from the climb as we decided to turn around and go back to the bottom. This initial climb was so strenuous that for the first time I wondered if I would be able to complete the climb to Kilimanjaro.

Charlie Wittmack giving us a pep talk.
Dr. Richard Deming is to his right.

MIDNIGHT MISERIES

AFTER SUPPER IT was dark, and everyone began to break out their lights. The lights were all of the new LED variety and the scene they created was like a field of fireflies. The little spots of light bounced everywhere as the group rustled about getting tents readied for the night. I was surprised that there were so few insects in the area, and since the evening was warm, getting the tent arranged was pleasant. My tent mate, Gail, proved to be a seasoned trekker. His duffle was orderly and he knew exactly how to arrange the tent space for maximum comfort and convenience. On the other hand, his tent mate would prove to be a bit trying.

Older men, especially older men who have had prostate cancer surgery and radiation, tend to have difficulty getting through the night without making several trips to the john. I'm one of them. I found the toilets just before retiring at about 7:00 p.m. So far so good; I went to sleep right away and by 10:00 p.m. I was awakened by the urge. I found my light and made my way to the toilet area amid the snores and growls of the mass of trekkers sleeping in their tents. There were tents, poles, ropes, rocks, and any number of other obstructions no matter which way I tried to pass. It wasn't easy, but I made it.

I got lost on the return trip and nearly entered a wrong tent. It seemed like all those obstacles were alive, and they were multiplying as I stumbled around the camp looking for some marker or distinctive feature on my tent. I eventually found my tent and after fumbling around for a few minutes I managed to get into my sleeping bag without waking Gail.

Like I said, nights for me require multiple trips to the john. My two a.m. urge was as expected. This time I decided that I wouldn't attempt the Tanzanian obstacle course, but I would avail myself of the device that Charlie had advised all of us to bring along on the trip. I found my light and went to the duffle bag looking for the plastic pee bottle that I bought at Walgreen's. This was when I learned the first rule of duffle bags. That is; "Anything that you are looking for in a duffle bag, always works its way to the bottom." By the time I found it, my urge was somewhere between pain and severe pain. Mission accomplished, I went back to bed. I was convinced that the idea of a pee bottle was a good one; I wouldn't stumble around in the darkness any more.

POLE, POLE

BEFORE BREAKFAST, MSGR. Frank Bognanno, a prostate cancer survivor, and a priest in the Diocese of Des Moines; celebrated Mass and I assisted as Deacon. About 20 people joined us for Mass. We set up a table to use as an altar and arranged our congregation inside the dining tent. It was crowded and jumbled, but it worked. I thought that this was a wonderful way to begin our trek to the top of Kilimanjaro. After last night's dinner and this morning's breakfast, I also wondered how long it would be before I had another good meal.

I have known Fr. Frank for about 30 years. He was my pastor for a while in the 80's. He was accompanied by his niece from Georgia, also a cancer survivor. It was good to have someone I know on the trip, we have a lot in common with respect to our ministries and we have many friends in common. I found his niece, Anna, to be enjoyable company. Fr. Frank and Anna became our evening entertainers with loads of good stories. Well, not always good stories, but always entertaining.

After Mass and breakfast, the climbers were divided into three groups with a guide for each group. Our guide was General Chombo and we began the trek with him in the lead. Before heading up the mountain, Chombo announced that we should try to drink at least 2 liters of water a day. "Water in; water out!" he exclaimed. "To be successful you have to drink lots of water." Then he announced in a loud bass voice, "Pole, Pole" (pronounced "Polie, Polie") Swahili for "Slow, Slow," and we were off.

The General set the pace. He would take small steps, slowly moving his large frame from one foot to the other. He carried a heavy pack on his back and had a single hiking pole in his right hand. His movement was undulating from side to side in a steady rhythm. He often repeated "Pole, Pole." The pace was good for me; even though I was struggling on the steep inclines as I had done the evening before, I was keeping up with the line. By the time we reached the flat section where we turned around the night before, I was breathing evenly. I was feeling more confident and I was comfortable moving in concert with the group.

Two hours later we came to another especially difficult climb. We were in the middle of the rain forest, and the rocks, roots, and high steps were again demanding. After climbing for about a mile; we descended for about a half mile over equally bad terrain. Then it was up again. Stepping over rocks, tree roots, deadfalls, and other obstructions was difficult; but I was making it.

Charlie came up to me and said he would carry my pack. At first I refused. I really wanted to carry my own pack and carry it all the way to our camp for the evening. Charlie insisted, and he took the pack while I rested for a moment. From this point on, I felt relief. The weight of the pack had slowed me considerably even though I didn't realize it. On the steep upgrades I would still breathe hard and struggle for breath, but once on a level, or nearly level, area; I would recover quickly.

While walking I thought of the many people I knew who had died of cancer or were currently in treatment for cancer. As I took a step I would say to myself, Uncle Eddie, Aunt Nora, or Cousin Elaine. I would then think of a saint that reminded me of that person, and with the next step I would ask that saint to "Pray for us." It was

Major General Chumbo

39

my own version of the "Pilgrim's Prayer." I walked and prayed in this manner each day. I surprised myself with the number of people I remembered: Uncle Ed, Aunt Nora, Uncle Lou, Uncle Dick, Cousins Elaine, Marjorie, and Joan; my childhood friend, Marilyn, my wife's uncle John, and my high school friends; Patty, Paul, Bill, and Joyce. My friend Dr. Bill Semon, who passed away recently of pancreatic cancer, and, of course; my brother, John, who died at age 70 with a glioblastoma, was especially on my mind. I reminded myself that I needed to call his wife, and check on my nieces and nephew by e-mail.

Time and space had separated me from my brother for many years. He had moved to Puerto Rico as a young man and we were not able to visit regularly. We had promised to spend more time together every time we talked. Retirement would mean more time for us to fish the Greenbrier, the Cranberry, and the Tygart; as we did as teenagers. Retirement would mean more time for nieces and nephews, retirement would mean that we would gather as family; and enjoy the presence of our spouses in laughter and happiness. It wasn't to be, cancer intervened and he died before retirement. I miss him terribly.

SARAH

I FIRST NOTICED Sarah at our exercise and yoga classes prior to the trip to Kilimanjaro. She is a tall, attractive 33 year old cancer survivor. Sarah is physically fit, strong, and personable. She tends to keep a bit to herself, but when you engage her in conversation she readily responds. During the yoga sessions, Sarah could master the positions, utilize weights, and maintain balance in a way that bespoke grace. I think that one of the reasons I liked Sarah was that she would laugh at my quips. Her laugh isn't a loud laugh, but one that has a statement behind it. Like, "Dave, that really isn't funny, but I'll laugh anyway."

Sarah is a thoughtful person. On her Face Book page she describes herself as a person who "thinks for herself." I believe that's accurate. At our second camp, Sarah climbed onto a tree trunk that was somewhat parallel to the ground, found a comfortable position, and surveyed the campground as she wrote her journal for the day.

When Sarah joined in conversation, she would use facial expressions to indicate her reactions. She could lift an eyebrow, tilt her head, or purse a lip; and people around her would understand the action. Not only is her face expressive, her posture is as well. She walks tall, with her shoulders back, and with a determined demeanor. It all comes together to say, "This woman knows who she is."

The campground was alive with activity. The porters were setting up the dinner tents and moving chairs and tables first one way and then another. The trekkers were gathered in groups and most were in animated conversation talking about what they had seen on the trail. People would move from group to group, pretty much leaving Sarah alone. Some, including me, took her picture; everyone tried not to disturb her. After about an hour, Sarah finished her journal entries and the tree became a favorite spot for others to climb onto for pictures.

Sarah Russell contemplating her journal.

After her successful climb of Mount Kilimanjaro, Sarah and our group visited an orphanage in town. Sarah immediately attracted some of the children. One of them reached up to Sarah asking to be picked up. Sarah held the child for a long time. They jostled and played, each enjoying the other as they walked across the playground. Their expressions spoke of an intimacy that is rarely found on such short notice.

Sarah with her new friend.

Sarah is just one of the cancer survivors I met on the trek to Kilimanjaro. Everyone was pleasant and helpful. Everyone was willing to pitch in and help others whenever they could. I wondered what Sarah was thinking on several occasions when another person talked about being a cancer survivor. I am hopeful that she will express some of those thoughts as we continue our friendship. It must be difficult to be a cancer patient at such an early age. Sarah exudes confidence and determination, and as a young woman with so much of life to live, and with all the challenges she must face; Sarah expressed for me one word: courage.

ON THE TRAIL

WE LEARNED TODAY that we wouldn't have access to a satellite phone, as planned, because the battery wasn't allowed on the plane flight from Amsterdam. I expressed my disappointment immediately to Gail. He didn't seem to mind. He simply said, "I told my wife that she wouldn't hear from me for a couple of weeks." His comment caught me by surprise. It wasn't a disrespectful comment at all. It was just a statement of fact. I understood right away, that as an experienced trekker, Gail had prepared his wife for his absence during the trek. I found myself wishing that I'd had that foresight.

The day's hiking had been spent in the rainforest and our camp for tonight was also in the rainforest. Fortunately the weather had been good and we walked all day in sunshine or clouds. We saw few animals. The birds we saw were small, occasional and often loud. This wasn't the rainforest as I had anticipated. We heard monkeys howl from time to time, but I only saw one monkey all day.

During the afternoon break from hiking, I had several conversations with other trekkers. I was asked by one man to describe some of the side effects of the hormone treatment that I am currently taking. It was as if he knew that this was something I would be uncomfortable talking about. He asked quietly, and then we stepped aside, away from others so our conversation was private. He was at the point of his treatment where he had to consider hormone therapy. I have been on hormone therapy for five years and this was the first time I'd talked about it with anyone other than my wife and a few close friends.

Dave's Hiking Group

I told him that impotence was almost a certainty. I also told him about the hot flashes that would come on suddenly, and that I had to take medication to counteract them. At first, my hot flashes were mostly at night. I would wake up with the sheets soaked in sweat. Usually, once I woke up I would be unable to go back to sleep. My doctors prescribed medication to help; it helped in that I did get much better rest, but the flashes continue. They are especially bothersome when I vest at Mass. With the heavy vestments I overheat so much that my glasses fog over. I just wait it out and I have never been compelled to leave the altar space because of these inconviences. I also told him that when I began to take the medication, I had feelings of disassociation. Once I became accustomed to the medication, these feelings went away. My doctor suggested an increased dosage, but as I regularly use woodworking and farming equipment, I declined. As long as I get a good night's sleep, I'm OK.

A few minutes later, we walked over to where Brian Triplett, our embedded reporter, was interviewing another cancer survivor. He was a recent cancer patient who had surgery only three weeks before our trip to Kilimanjaro, and he was telling Brian about his experience. This was something that I had been unable to do except for family and a few close friends for 23 years. I was surprised at how easily I was able to join in the conversation. It was as if a burden had been lifted and I had "come out" of a period of stagnation. These men were experiencing some of the same thoughts and feelings that I had over the years. I was not alone.

Rain Forest Trees covered with Moss.

THE SHIRA PLATEAU

WE LEFT CAMP on day three in clear weather. Initially the walking was much like the day before, but we had a new guide, Charlie. Charlie set the pace a bit quicker than the General. After about an hour, both Nina and I were falling back. Charlie settled into his pace, and; rather than walk "pole, pole," as the General did, he would stop and wait for us to catch up. Charlie was a lithe man of 28. He was married and had several children. His English wasn't as good as the General's but with effort we could communicate.

By mid-morning we approached a steep rise in elevation. At first the forest would have some breaks where sunlight would come to the ground. These open areas gradually became larger and larger until we were walking in shrubs that stretched to the horizon. The shrubs were all about six to eight feet tall and gradually gave way to a steady height of four to six feet. Just after noon we came to a level area that was cluttered with large rounded boulders. These boulders were from one or two feet in diameter to as large as thirty feet in diameter. As we crossed over the level area we started up a rise that soon became a steep steady climb. As we mounted this climb, the boulders were left behind us.

In geological theory, these boulders were large molten or semi molten blobs of volcanic lava that this now dormant volcano threw up 500,000 or more years ago. This lava then formed into spherical shapes as they traveled in the cold air above the clouds. They fell onto the slope of previously congealed lava and rolled down to gather on the level space. These boulders rest today more than 20 miles from the Kilimanjaro caldera.

Today, Mike, a cancer survivor who makes his living as a kick boxer, came up behind me and took my pack. He simply reached out and gently took the pack off my back with a, "Hey, Dave, let me carry that a while." Mike walked behind me for several hours as we made our way up. He is a physically fit, strong athlete. He responds to inquiries about his profession in a straight forward way, but there isn't a hint of bravado. I was especially appreciative of his constant encouragement as our line moved up the serpentine trail.

We expected to be in camp by 4:00 p.m. This would give us more time to socialize and rest before supper. We continued to climb higher and higher. At 4 p.m. I asked our guide how much longer before we made camp. "Ten minutes." He responded. "Piece of cake," I thought. Two hours later, after more climbing, we rounded a bend and Kilimanjaro was before us reflecting the rays of the setting sun.

Kilimanjaro above the Shira Plateau, 20 miles away.

It was well after dark before we came into camp. We came in singing the Kilimanjaro song that Charlie, the guides, and the porters had taught us. Those in camp responded with cheers. I had planned to assist at Mass and give the homily, but because we were so late Fr. Frank had already finished Mass.

Kilimanjaro Song

Jambo	*Hello*
Jambo Bwana	*Hello Mr.*
Habari Gani	*How are you today?*
Nzum Sana	*Very Good!*
Laoeni	*Guests/Visitors*
Mwakawi Bishwa	*Have Lots of Energy for . . .*
Kilimanjaro	*Kilimanjaro*
Hakuna Matata	*No Problem*

I FILLED MY water bottles as soon as I came into camp and quenched my thirst. Supper was late and consisted of cold spaghetti and an herb sauce that wasn't very palatable. I did get down some of the spaghetti and some fruit, but I didn't really feel hungry. I drank a half liter of water as I remembered the General's admonition. Since there was nothing else to do, I went to bed.

My miseries continued. Now that I was comfortable using the pee bottle, I wasn't too worried about having to make midnight rounds to the john. I was right on schedule; ten, two, and four. The problem this time was that after 4:00 a.m. the bottle was full. I couldn't lay it down or it would pour out. I used my light and found a way to brace the bottle against a rock and packed some of my clothing around it to hold it in place. "I'll take it outside in the morning," I thought, and I crawled into my sleeping bag.

My wife tells me that I'm a fitful sleeper. She also tells me that I snore. Gail will testify that I snore, so I can't deny it. Sometime during the night, in my restlessness, I kicked over the bottle. All of the clothing that was supporting it was saturated. Even with the clothing saturated, there was a big puddle in the bottom of the tent. I cleaned up the puddle using other garments and all of my pads. I then used all of my hand sanitizer to sanitize the tent floor as best I could. All the while, Gail was patient and didn't say a word; even when I used words that deacons should never use. From that moment, I dubbed him, "Saint Gail."

We woke to a cold morning. Frost covered the ground and clung to the stems of brush. At first I thought that we had a coating of snow, but when the cold air hit my face I realized it was frost. The ground at the Shira Plateau Camp was wet and rocky. It was difficult to find an area where the ground was dry. With sunup, the wind picked up and the cold intensified. Once we started our daily Yoga exercise, we warmed up, and as the sun rose it cleared the frost away making for comfortable hiking. My breakfast was a small bowl of porridge, cold toast, and honey.

The honey in Tanzania is darker, thicker and stickier than the honey we buy in an Iowa supermarket. It also has a stronger flavor. It is especially good on toast, or it can be used to sweeten coffee or tea. On our first day in Tanzania, I noticed a honeybee drawing nectar from a flower. The honeybee was definitely an African honeybee. The bee was darker, slimmer and slightly smaller than the honeybees that are tended in the US. I once kept bees with a friend in West Virginia, and our bees were of the type usually referred to as "European," or "blond" honeybees. I am curious to know if the honey we had in Africa was from wild or domestic hives. It is a brave soul that would keep the African bee, or raid a wild colony of these aggressive bees. These are the bees that escaped from a research project in Brazil about 1930, gradually moved up the Isthmus of Panama, through Mexico, and are found today in Southern Texas. We refer to them as "killer bees." It is interesting that the original African bees that researchers took to Brazil for study were captured in Tanzania.

The porters broke camp and immediately started preparing their loads to move us to the next camp. The porters are amazing. They carry up to 33lbs and by regulation, no more. The porters are mostly in their 20's, but a few are in their early thirties. They are agile, surefooted, and can carry their loads; plus their personal backpack, from one camp to another faster than we can hike the trail. Some leave before sunup and will make two trips. Others will leave after us, and they will pass us on the trail and be busy setting up camp before we arrive. These men not only work hard, but the General told me that the work pays well and that there is a lot of competition to be a porter on his crew. Most of them speak some English and they are cheerful and friendly at all times.

Day Three

I began day three with a great deal of optimism. I was keeping up with the group and felt good as we walked over some rough ground and then crossed several streams. The stream crossings were delicate but doable; and I managed without getting my feet wet or falling. At one point, I began to stumble and was headed for the drink, but Steve reached back and gave me a hand. About halfway through the morning I felt a growling in my stomach. At first I didn't think much about it but about an hour later the growling became a cramp. At our next rest stop, I had to find a rock away from the others to relieve the cramping. As I re-joined the group, I remembered hearing Charlie telling us that the water we filled up on the evening before hadn't been boiled as long as it should have been. I took a Loperamide pill and continued on. I didn't have another attack of diarrhea the rest of the day. I thought I was out of the woods; or should I say "rocks?"

We got into camp about 3:15. The climbing had been hard and the rise steep. I was pretty tired so I lay down for a while to take a nap. Lunch had yet to be served so my plan was to eat well at lunch and skip supper. My duffle wasn't in camp yet, so my nap was on the ground pad without a sleeping bag. It was surprisingly comfortable as the sun was warming the tent and the tent was breaking the wind.

We were now only a two day hike from the top of Kilimanjaro. My nap had invigorated me and I managed to find some toast and honey to eat. I also ate one of the high protein bars I carried in my backpack. I found some time to commiserate with several of our fellow travelers, and I heard that because we were a bit late on the trail, we would take a different approach to the top. We were also told that the original trail had been deemed "too dangerous" by park officials because of storms, freezing, and thawing.

Just before supper, Fr. Frank set up a table for Mass. I got my alb and stole and went to join him. We celebrated the Feast of Epiphany with a large crowd. Some of the porters joined us, and; after Mass, Fr. Frank offered the Sacrament of the Sick to everyone. I was grateful for this opportunity as I knew that the bad water I had the night before could easily cost me the opportunity to reach the top. It was nearly 7:00 pm when we finished Mass and the Sacrament of the Sick. I stuck to my plan of skipping dinner and went into the tent and went to bed. I had been doing fine since mid-morning when I took the Loperamide. I fell into a deep sleep right away.

Sometime around 10:00 p.m. I became aware of some cramping in my stomach. At first it was no more than a nuisance that brought me to half-awake consciousness. I rolled over onto my side and pulled my knees up toward my chin. I was aware that I was chasing sleep and that the cramping was gradually intensifying. Suddenly I was wide awake and the cramping was as if I had serpents coiling inside me. I got out of the sleeping bag as quick as I could and searched for my flashlight and shoes. As soon as I pulled on my shoes I began my dash for the toilet tent.

I made it about 10 yards before I was forced to stop right where I was and sit on the side of a rock. In the process I soiled my clothes and shoes. I was petrified that someone would awaken and come out of their tent to see me in the altogether. I made my way back to the tent, checked to be sure no one was around, took off my shoes and the rest of my clothes, and re-entered the tent just as naked as I was in the dark changing room three months earlier.

The cold of the night was piercing through me and I began to shiver. I rummaged through my duffle and found some clean clothes. While I was putting on my clothes I felt cramping in the back of my legs and calves. I'm told that in life and business; height is an asset. That isn't true in a tent.

Each tent had a vestibule where we kept our duffels and backpacks, and a sleeping area for a ground pad and our sleeping bag. The tent is no more than 4 feet tall at its tallest. There's no center pole as the tent is supported by metal hoops, with ropes and ground stakes on the outside. With nothing to hold onto for support, I had to sit on my haunches while searching for clothing in the duffle. After only a few minutes, the position caused the backs of my legs and calves to curl in pain. I hurriedly put on whatever I could find and crawled back to the sleeping bag. In the sleeping area, my head would be against the far wall of the tent and my feet would extend over the flap into the vestibule area. The warmth of the bag soothed me and I went back to sleep.

Within an hour the serpents returned. It felt as if my insides were twisting and turning and pressure was descending. At this signal I made a dash for the toilet, and again I was stopped only a few yards from my tent. And so the night went; my entire body was out of control and out of sync. By morning I had made the trip at least a half dozen times. All this time, Gail slept quietly, or at least he pretended to.

Gail rose early, dressed and left the tent. After a few minutes I heard Dr. Hyatt's voice asking through the tent, "Dave, how are you doing?" My answer was a weak, "Not very good." I got out of the sleeping bag and prepared for another trip to the john. Dr. Hyatt and Dr. Deming were both at the tent entrance. I stumbled coming out of the tent. They caught me under the arms and assisted me toward the toilet. I didn't make it, and another set of clothes was soiled. After I got back to the tent opening, one of them asked me what medicines I was taking. In my confusion I couldn't remember and stammered a bit. Dr. Deming asked me if I wanted to go on, and I read into his voice that he had doubts that I should. I answered, "No." I regret that decision to this day, but the die was cast as the rest of the encampment prepared to move forward.

They helped me undress in the vestibule. I was shivering through and through as I tried to get some clean clothing on. I crawled into the sleeping bag and Dr. Deming helped me pull on clean shorts. My shivering by now was a trembling, almost violent, shaking. Dr. Hyatt came in and helped me get down two Loperamide capsules. I was thirsty and I drank water from my water bottle not caring whether or not it was tainted. After Dr. Hyatt left I continued to shiver. A few minutes later I heard a voice.

"Dave, can I come in?" It was Mary. She came in with hardly a rustle, and knelt down beside me. She leaned over and put her cheek next to mine. "I failed." I thought, and then I said it out loud, "Mary, I failed." "No, Dave, you didn't fail; it could have happened to any one of us," she said. I was aware of tears on my cheeks; both her's and mine. Mary got up and left the tent as noiselessly as she had entered.

A few moments later I heard another voice. It was Fr. Frank. "Dave," he called from outside the tent. "A number of us have gathered around the tent to offer a blessing." I responded, but I'm not sure what I said. Fr. Frank then prayed for me, asking God the Father, Son, and Spirit to assist me off the mountain and deliver me to good health. As he prayed I could hear the others praying along in soft voices. I felt warmth over my chest and a relaxing of the shivers. At the end of the prayer I summoned my best voice to respond to my colleagues' prayer. I intoned with as much force as I could muster:

"Praise God from Whom All Blessings Flow,
Praise him you creatures here below,
Praise Him above you heavenly hosts,
Praise Father, Son, and Holy Ghost."

At the conclusion of this Great Doxology, I heard an "Amen," followed by footsteps moving toward the trail.

I settled once again into a semi sleep. My upper body was now warm and calm. My knees and feet were still shaking with cold. I tried to put the cold out of my mind so I could sleep and gather some strength for the walk down the mountain to a jeep road about 30 minutes away. Just as I was drifting into a deeper sleep, I felt someone massaging my feet. I could feel the warmth flow from my knees to my feet as the massaging continued for several minutes. I shook the sleep, and raised my head just enough to see who it was. It was General Chombo. "You go down now, Pa, Pa." he said, using the African phrase of respect for "Grandfather." He helped me get my shoes on, pack my gear, and then assisted me as I rose to come out into the sunlight. I was joined by Nina and Dee, both of whom had decided to return to Moshe.

The walk down the mountain to the pickup point was more like two hours than a half hour. The first half mile and the last half mile were the most difficult. The guide (Charlie) helped us when the steps were high or when we had to cross a stream or a gully. The walk was somber, with little talking. There were four other porters with us. One had a sprained ankle and two were just as sick as me. The fourth was, for an unspoken reason, going off duty. The fact that even the porters could become ill or be injured helped me to realize that I may not be such a wimp after all.

There were some other porters at the pickup point when we arrived, and within minutes everyone was in the Jeep. It wasn't really a Jeep, that's what they called it; it was a Land Rover with a large bed in the back. All of our duffels were put in the back and Dee climbed into the bed with the porters. They sat on top of the duffels in order to have a soft ride. Nina was up front with me. The ride back to the entrance of the park was about two hours of lurching, bumping and bouncing. We re-crossed all of the environmental zones we had walked through during the previous days. Once at the entrance we had to sign out before we could go on to Moshe.

When we arrived at the hotel the receptionist was waiting for us. The hotel owner came out to greet us and make sure that we were comfortable. She even offered to take us to the hospital if we had the need. At this point I was dog tired and all I wanted was an ice cold Coke followed by a bed. I napped until 5:00 p.m., and then I started washing my clothes in the basin of the hotel room. I hung my clothes on the railing outside my room following the example of other guests. I then cleaned my duffle and back pack, showered, and got ready for dinner.

Dinner was at 7:30, much too late for my stomach. I had a small helping of prawns over rice, a little bit of fruit and another Coke. The prawns were in a light cream sauce that was excellent. Too bad I was afraid to have more. I went back to my room, took some more Loperamide, and retired. I slept well and was up early when a new Chanticleer provided his serenade outside my window.

The hotel was on a deep rutted dirt road and is inside a walled enclave. There is a guard at the entrance gate armed with a knife that looked like a machete, but a little shorter. He wore it in a leather scabbard that was decorated with red, white and blue, stitching. The guard was a large man in his mid thirties and he looked like he and the machete were made to match. The walls of the enclave were topped with concertina wire and had an additional strand of barbed wire running above for the entire the length of the wall.

Inside the hotel was a large courtyard divided into four unequal sections. Each section had a slightly different arrangement of tables, umbrellas, or wooden coverings to provide shade. The sections were divided by walks lined with shrubs and flowers. The largest section was the bar area that was subdivided into smoking and non smoking. On this day, my second at the hotel, I found a comfortable chair under a covering and finished the book I had been saving for the plane ride.

I ran into Dee about lunchtime and we discussed the possibility of a safari tour the next day. By this time I was feeling like I should be back up on the mountain, and I was wondering if I hadn't jumped the gun on my decision to abandon the trek. Anyway, done was done, so I began to look forward to the safari. I ate well this day, but I was still afraid to stop taking the Loperamide.

I spent an hour or so in the bar before dinner. I tested my innards with my first beer since coming off the mountain. As I sat in the bar area there was an activity that caught my eye. I saw guides meeting with clients and witnessed their negotiations as they planned their treks to Mount Kilimanjaro. The guides were obviously experienced businessmen. They used maps and calculators, and then drew up contracts on the spot. Sometimes there were as few as two people negotiating with a guide and sometimes there might be three or four couples along with some porters. Once the negotiation was completed, the guide, or one of his porters, would take the contract and go to the hotel office to make everyone a copy. When the copies came back the parties would stand up, shake hands, and be on their way until the agreed upon meeting time. These negotiations were all done in English, regardless of the nationality of the trekkers. I witnessed negotiations by Danes, Germans, Austrians, Swedes, Aussies, and Brits. I know that eavesdropping is impolite, but this was too much fun to miss. I think I felt a little bit like Humphrey Bogart in Casablanca.

Courtyard at Springlands Hotel. Notice the guide and trekkers negotiating at the table at top right.

SAFARI

THE NEXT DAY we went to Arusha National Park to view some African wildlife. Our guide and driver was James. James was an older man who was experienced as a naturalist. He was a pleasant person who did his best to make sure that we had a good day. We entered Arusha National Park about 10:30 a.m. and were greeted by a small herd of giraffes practically at the entrance.

Water buck in Arusha National Park.

The park was immense. We rode in the truck all day and saw a wide variety of wildlife; Zebras, baboons, monkeys, flamingos, giraffes, warthogs, water buffalo, dik diks, African eagles, and water bucks. My favorite was a water buck that was close to our van for several minutes.

We returned to the Hotel at 5:00 p.m. I went to the bar and began to eavesdrop again. This time the scene was different. There were two men with a guide and two porters settling their account after a trek. I'll call the men Mutt and Jeff. The taller man was the lead negotiator and the shorter man, although he could be described as stocky, not round, was quietly allowing Mutt to settle up. They were in complete agreement as to the final bill; Mutt pulled out his billfold and paid the guide in full. They immediately broke from a business mode to a social mode. Mutt ordered a beer for everyone. Jeff came out of his quiet persona and engaged in conversation with the guide and porters. It was evident that it had been a successful trek and that everyone was happy.

Mutt and Jeff were from California, but they both spoke with a New York accent. They were in their trekking clothes; dirty and unshaven. The guide and porters were also ready for a shower and a good night's sleep. But the party continued. They had a second beer, and then a third. I was still on my first. After an hour all five men stood, shook hands and bid farewell. These men, two New Yorkers who now lived in California, and three Africans who had provided them with a service, were now connected for a lifetime. I wondered if they would ever see one another again. I also wondered if I would have an opportunity to see Charlie, General Chombo, and the other porters on my trek again. After a few minutes I ordered a second beer and began to think about all of the people who had been a part of my life for the past week.

James our guide on Safari.

The courtyard of the hotel was delightful, with palm trees, flowers with red, white, and yellow blooms, and decorated walkways. The people were wonderful and the beer was good. After the safari I spent a day reading and talking with other guests. I met a man from Denmark, Arne, who was an airline pilot and also worked part time for the hotel as a recruiter in Charlotte, North Carolina.

We talked about the difficulties of Tanzania with respect to infrastructure and employment. He was knowledgeable about the country as he had been working for the hotel for a number of years. He told me that the people of Tanzania, represented by a number of tribes, were a hard working people who were forced to rely on their own wits for employment. Inflation, government ineptitude, and lack of infrastructure had pretty much destroyed any manufacturing.

Arne was well known to many of the hotel guests and staff. He kept up a steady conversation with whoever was near. During our conversations, he asked me if I had been up the mountain. I admitted to him that I didn't make it past the 14,000 foot level and that I was a bit bummed out. He responded immediately that he thought I'd done pretty well. "More than most people who live here." He went on to explain that the local lore is that anyone who goes up the mountain, even if they don't top out, can call her "Kili."

The infrastructure of Tanzania is poor by any standard. There are very few paved roads and the ones that are paved are only two lanes and are in desperate need of repair. Most of the road to Kilimanjaro National Park, a major source of revenue for the tourist industry, was abysmal. Other roads are even worse. There are some sewers but no sewage treatment, no source of potable water, no central garbage collection, poor public schools, and electric power is often operating on brown out, or off completely. My friend told me that there are no property taxes and that the economy is basically a barter economy with only 8% of people paying any taxes at all. The next morning, Thursday January 12, 2012, I was to learn more about the people and the culture of Tanzania.

JONATHAN

TODAY, NINA, DEE and I will move to a new hotel
downtown. This hotel, we are told, is an upscale hotel that
is air conditioned. This is the hotel where the entire group
will come when their trek is over. It is where we will hold
our parting farewell to Tanzania on Saturday evening.

The hotel shuttle picked us up about 9:30 a.m. There
was a young lady from Lincoln, Nebraska, already on board.
She was about 22 years old, a recent college graduate, and
she was a volunteer teacher serving with a nongovernmental
organization in Kenya. I asked her where she was headed
and she gave me a rundown of her plans.

She was on holiday and had decided to travel to Dar Es
Salam, to meet some friends. We chatted for a while and
I asked her if she was concerned about her safety while
traveling in Tanzania. "Oh, no," She replied. "I've travelled
all over by bus and sometimes by car with the locals. This
is really a cool place." When we got to town center she
hopped out, grabbed her backpack and trotted toward
the bus station. "Be careful" I called after her. 'I will,'" she

71

answered. I was feeling better about my plans to do some exploring of my own.

Hotel Panama is located just off the main street and market. After checking in I watched CNN for about an hour to catch up on the news. When CNN began to repeat itself, I decided to have lunch and go for a walk in the marketplace. I asked the receptionist at the front desk if it was safe for me to go out into the market by myself. He assured me that I would be OK as long as "you mind your own business," whatever that meant.

The market in Moshe is extensive. There are kiosks, stands, storefronts, carts, and vendors galore. Everything needed for local consumption and every sort of tourist knick knack is offered for sale in the shops, on the streets, and from carts and automobiles. I noted my location carefully so as not to get lost and started walking up and down the streets. The smells of ripe pineapple, charcoal fires, sawdust, and dirt mixed to provide a new sensory experience. There were plumbing stores, hardware stores, metal stores, motorbike stores, food markets, currency exchangers, banks, butchers, and fish markets. All of these were mixed in with dress shops, hat shops, and souvenir offerings of all descriptions. I had made up my mind that I would buy my wife and daughters-in-law each a dress made from some of the beautiful fabrics I saw the local women wearing.

Tanzanian women dress in a variety of ways depending on tribe, religion, or geographical location. Some wear dresses that are spectacular. The fabric is light, usually polyester, with every color imaginable: Reds, yellows, purple, browns, blues, greens, orange, or any combination. The colors are sometimes like a tie die tee shirt, or they can be stripes, blotches, or lines. The dresses remind me of a Jackson Pollack mural. Whatever the colors or design, there is always a pleasing pattern. The dresses are worn loose and the material falls gracefully. Older women wear the dresses with one side a little bit higher above the ankles. Younger women wear them to just below the knee.

I walked for over an hour observing the dress shops and noting their locations so I could narrow my shopping to four or five stores. I stopped in one shop and discovered the dresses were all labeled "Made in Indonesia," "Made in India," or some other country. I wanted dresses "Made in Tanzania," or I wouldn't buy anything. I left the shop wondering if I could find what I was looking for.

I turned down a side street where there were stacks of pineapple, avocado, mango, bananas and papaya. The fragrance was delightful. One vendor offered to cut a watermelon for me. I declined, remembering my mountain misery of a few days before. The sides of the street were lined with small shops and goods were hanging from anything, even the poles that supported the roof. There were several shops displaying colorful dresses and fabrics.

Just as I started toward a shop, a young man came beside me and fell into step. "Hi," he said. "What are you looking for? Maybe I can help." At first I politely declined, but he persisted. "My name is Jonathan, and you are?" I told him my name and he asked me again what I was looking for. I told him I was looking for some dresses for the ladies in my life. He smiled and said, "Come with me, I know where to go."

Jonathan was about 5 feet nine or ten, slim, and handsome. His complexion was slightly lighter than the dark chocolate of most of the people in Moshe, and his English was excellent. He smiled easily and his eyes flashed. He was dressed in blue jeans, and a dull yellow short-sleeve shirt. He looked as if he could have been a student at any American college or university.

He led me across the street, past some stacked pineapples, and into a small shop. The shop was no larger than ten feet by ten feet. There was a glass showcase just inside and the room had a wooden floor. The showcase held various knick knacks and doo dads. An older lady was behind the case and about two feet behind her was a rack with dozens of dresses. The floor on the lady's side of the showcase was dirt and the walls were covered with shelves loaded with bolts of fabric. Jonathan immediately launched into conversation with the lady in Swahili. The lady got up and started pulling dresses off of the rack behind her. The colorful prints were terrific; just what I was looking for. I reached for the one that caught my eye the most, and held it up as if I were measuring it for myself. I looked under the collar and found a tag. It said, "Made in Indonesia."

Disappointed, I handed the dress to Jonathan and emphasized that I wanted something made in Tanzania. Jonathan handed the dress to the lady and spoke again in Swahili. The lady nodded in understanding, and I could tell by her expression that all of her dresses were made in Indonesia.

"I know a place where I'm sure you can get what you want." Jonathan said. "Do you mind walking a ways?" "No," I answered. He pulled out a cell phone and made a call. I reckoned that he was talking to another shop owner, probably someone he knew. The conversation lasted only a few minutes. When he ended the call, he again spoke to the shop owner in Swahili, then he thanked her and said "Goodbye" in English. He motioned to me, smiled, and said, "Come."

We started out side by side, Jonathan talking non-stop. He told me that he was 20 years old and had been to school at the "University." He told me he lived with his mom, dad, and five sisters, and that he was the eldest. We walked back to the main street, past the Hotel Panama and further on toward the west. As we walked I noticed that the street became less and less of a market place and more and more like a commercial business district. We walked by a bank where there were two men outside, each carrying automatic rifles. They were dressed in Army green and they walked back and forth in front of the bank. Just past the bank, the sidewalk narrowed, but there were still a lot of people about.

Three blocks later the commercial character of the neighborhood began to change to residential. The residences were small, one or two room structures that appeared to have stone floors. I could see that some had a cooking area in the back. By this time I was walking behind Jonathan in order to navigate the narrowing walk and dodge the oncoming people at the same time. I was also becoming suspicious. I fell behind Jonathan about ten feet and determined that I wouldn't enter any building where I couldn't see in. I wanted to be sure that I wouldn't get into a situation where I couldn't find a way out. Jonathan kept going; turning around from time to time to be sure I was there. A few minutes after I fell behind him he stopped talking and was just leading.

We turned down a side street. There were no shops or vendors evident on this street. The street was narrower than the street where we had been. There were people sitting on small porches, and there was a lot of conversation; many spoke to Jonathan as if they knew him. We stopped in front of a small building that had a porch built right to the edge of the street. Jonathan called out in Swahili. When the door opened I could see that the room beyond was full of dresses. The lady inside came out and invited us in. She introduced me to her husband and daughter who were just inside the door.

The daughter was dressed in a spectacular garment. It was multicolored, with prints and other decorations that were eye stopping. In addition to the colors, the dress had a gold liner across the top and a similar decoration along the bottom hem. She was a beautiful girl, and I would guess that she was about 16. The lady was explaining to me, through Jonathan, that the drape of the dress, where one side is lifted above the ankle slightly; is accomplished by wearing a belt under the dress and then gathering a portion of fabric and tucking it in with the belt.

The lady and her daughter modeled my selections for size, and I soon picked out four dresses. Then the negotiation began. The lady spoke through Jonathan and offered the four dresses for $250. I countered with $160. Jonathon rebutted with $220 and I made my final offer at $200. The lady looked downcast. Her lips pouted, her eyes fell and her shoulders sagged. It was an international language that we were speaking, and I thought about how bartering and negotiating had been accomplished over centuries by peoples who spoke different languages. Finally, Jonathon, without consulting the lady, offered. "Meet you in the middle, $210?" I hesitated a moment, then said, "Deal:" and extended my hand. Heads came up, smiles were on every face, and we shook hands all around.

I walked back to the hotel happy with my purchase, but at the same time sad for Jonathan, the lady, her husband and their daughter. I have had a good life, I have lived in the best of times and I have had the best medical care in the world. My life has been extended so I could visit Moshe, Tanzania, and enjoy meeting such good people: But what about them? What if any one of them would be stricken with cancer? What kind of medical care could they get? Would they even know about their cancer in time to have effective treatment? Or, would they simply keep working day by day until the disease invaded their systems followed by a slow and painful death? My grandson, Theodore, is the same age as Jonathon. Both young men are bright and capable, yet one will have many advantages and one will not. Where's the justice in that?

WELCOME BACK

THE HOTEL HAD been quiet all afternoon. Finally, about 6:30 p. m., I heard loud voices and the tramping of feet. The trekkers were back. I felt a comfort knowing that I would be with friends again. Cory and Tim came into the room and announced that everyone had made it to the top of Kili. They moved slowly and their tired bodies slumped. Both wanted a shower right away. Each told me his story as he waited for the other to clean up. Then both lay down to rest. I left the room and joined some others for a beer in the dining room. The other trekkers joined us gradually and dinner was served at about 9:30 p.m. Since most had grabbed a nap before dinner, there was a spontaneous party until late in the night. My own emotions at this time were mixed. I was happy to see everyone, but I still had a sense of failure. I wanted to experience that feeling of completion that they had and shared. All I could do was to listen and join them in their successes.

The next morning our group gathered to board busses to visit some local schools. When we went outside to get on the busses, Jonathan was there with a cadre of other vendors. All of them held their wares right in front of our faces. They were persistent and it was a challenge to walk around a bus to get on. Once on the bus the vendors would go to the open windows and push their wares through in an attempt to negotiate even if the passengers ignored them. Jonathan kept calling my name and he would point me out to the others. I'm sure he was telling them that I was the guy who bought the dresses the day before. It was near chaos before the busses finally left for our day trip.

The day trip consisted of stops at three schools and an orphanage. St Louis School was our first stop. It is a private elementary school operated by the Catholic Diocese of Moshe. We had an interview with the superintendant in one of the classrooms. She explained the school system in Tanzania, and was proud of her students' accomplishments on the exam that each 7th grader must pass in order to enter the 8th grade in the public school system. The students must pass a second exam after the 10th grade in order to go on to finish high school. There is also an exam to qualify for admittance to the University.

In Tanzania the title of "teacher" is highly regarded. Each teacher we met was addressed respectfully as "teacher" by both students and adults. There was a large segment of St. Louis School that was still under construction. The superintendant told us that as money became available, the unfinished floors would be finished and that they would eventually add high school grades to their curriculum.

Our second stop was at a public grade school. The difference was startling. The public grade school was more of an open air shed of a building, unlike the private school building that was more like an American grade school of the 1950's. At the public school, we were not greeted by any of the teachers or administrators. Rather, we made a considerable commotion by walking onto the play area unannounced.

The children were friendly like all Tanzanians. They crowded around us and wanted to have their pictures taken. They loved to make faces and assume silly postures for us to photograph, and then, with our digital cameras, they could see the resulting picture of themselves. Some of the kids would ask for money, but we had been advised not to give one child money; unless we were willing to give each child the same amount.

Education in Tanzania is expensive. The private Catholic School costs about $4000 a year. The public school is advertized as "free" but the fees for books, desk space, uniforms, and many others, make it almost as expensive as the private school. The result is that many children don't go to school at all. In rural areas, very few children go to school.

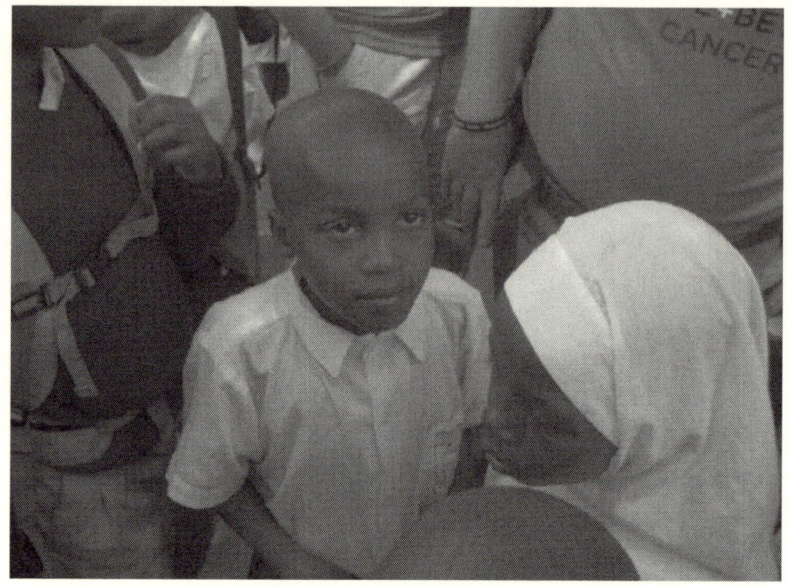

This boy begged me for money at the public school yard.

The final two stops were at the pre-school and orphanage that Teacher Edward Lazaro established in 2009. Like most of Africa, Tanzania has been hit very hard by the AIDS epidemic. Unfortunately, most of the victims of AIDS are people in their 20's, 30's, and 40's. There is little treatment for this disease in much of Africa. The result is that many people die at a young age and their children are left without anyone to care for them. The African culture emphasizes the family's responsibility to care for orphaned children, but since most people of child bearing age are infected by the AIDS virus, the extended family is often unable to provide for nieces and nephews who are orphaned.

Dr. Gary Higgins, a retired physician from Northern California, has assisted Lazaro for some time. As the children aged, Lazaro and Higgins saw the need for the pre-school. They founded the pre-school so the orphans would be ready to enter elementary school without being at a disadvantage. Lazaro recruits his teachers, and raises money to keep the orphanage and pre-school open and operating. When a child finishes pre-school, he or she goes to the public school, but continues to live at the orphanage. There are presently 39 orphans, ages 2-17, living under the care and guidance of Dr. Higgins and Teacher Edward.

Our visit to the orphanage was overwhelming. The children performed for us by singing and acting. The staff prepared a meal for us and we played with the children for a couple of hours. They were mannerly, well cared for and evidently healthy. They loved playing a form of "Ring around the Rosie," swinging, see-sawing, and patty-caking." The smaller children wanted to be held. One little boy sat beside me for about 20 minutes and just held my hand. "Where is the justice?", I thought, "I've had a good life, and a long life. I want these children to enjoy the same."

The boy on the left sat beside me and held my hand.

WINDING IT UP

SATURDAY WAS A day each person did pretty much what he or she wanted to do. Most slept to catch up after the arduous trek to the top of Kili. I wandered around town with a group, finishing up my shopping. I bought three small paintings for my sons, decorative bracelets for my granddaughters, and warrior bracelets for my grandsons.

My mind at this point was beginning to move toward home. I've missed my wife, children, and grandchildren. I kept drawing parallels and tangents about my life and the lives of these wonderful people. I asked myself, "Why they don't hate us?" They have been enslaved, colonized, cheated out of their land, and relegated to a life of service and poverty. Yet they welcome us; they want to speak our language; they want to engage in commerce; they are strong, healthy and intelligent. They have been denigrated as lazy, backward, and stupid, which they are not. These are a great people in a great land, a land with enormous possibilities. I was longing for home and at the same time I was longing to keep my new friends in my mind's eye. I prayed that I would never forget the goodness of the

General, Charlie (the guide), the ladies in the dress shop, the girl who modeled my wife's new dress, Jonathan, and the porters and vendors.

I also prayed that I would never forget those who accompanied me on this trip to Mount Kilimanjaro. They are people who share a part of my life. They have also either experienced cancer, were caregivers, or related to friends of cancer survivors, or; those who lost their lives to cancer. All have become a part of my life and they are all wound up in this person I call "me."

The plane out of Kilimanjaro was the same airplane that carried us into Kilimanjaro. It flies daily from Amsterdam to Kilimanjaro, to Dar Es Salam, and back to Amsterdam. The plane may be the same and the route may be nothing more than a big circle, but the people inside are all different. They are male and female. They are black and white; they are from many different continents and races. They are people with differing backgrounds and differing ideas and opinions. Some are young and some are old. Some are sick, some are well, and some are wealthy and some are poor. They are all people moving in the stream of life and doing their best to honor one another as citizens of this world. They may be strangers to one another, or best of friends, but there is one thing for certain; they are human beings on a course from birth to death.

When the plane landed in Amsterdam, I found something to eat and something to read. I'd slept a bit from Dar Es Salam, something that is unusual for me on an airplane. I knew that it was unlikely that I would sleep more on the ride from Amsterdam to Minneapolis. It would be a long trip and it would be in darkness most of the way.

After boarding the plane in Amsterdam, I found my seat and settled in. As I became comfortable, I saw Sarah coming down the aisle. When she was about ten feet away, her eyes caught mine. She cocked her head to the left, smiled and then shifted her eyes to the seat beside me. I knew right away that she would be my seatmate to Minneapolis. Once aloft, the available light was poor and the cabin was uncomfortable. Sarah put on her MP3 player and was asleep in just a few minutes.

Airplanes cramp me, and this one was worse than most. I tried to keep still to avoid disturbing her, but I'm just not very good at keeping still. I put away my book, removed my shoes and stretched my left leg into the aisle and my right leg under the seat in front of me as far I could. I was watching the plane progress across the North Atlantic on the monitor in front of me, and my mind began to roam.

My grandchildren range in age from 9 to 23. All are in good health. One is a college graduate; three are in college, three in high school, and two in grade school. How would I react if one of them were to be diagnosed with cancer? I have always pictured people with cancer to be old; and, well; my age.

Cancer is referred to as "The big C" and with diagnosis comes the expectation that death can't be far behind. I have spent more than two weeks with 18 cancer survivors who demonstrated that this just isn't the case. Sarah is one of them. She worked hard to be in good physical condition. She pushed herself through sickness, cold, and heat to get to the top of Kili. If one of my granddaughters were diagnosed with cancer, I would want her to know someone like Sarah. I would want them to talk about their condition and I would want them to be friends, just as I feel friendship with every person in this group. I would want my granddaughter to know that there is life after cancer and that with the right attitude, nutrition, and fitness, she would have an opportunity to live a productive and happy life.

I know that cancer treatment doesn't come with a guarantee. Some people respond to treatment and some don't. Sometimes cancer strikes early in life and sometimes it strikes late. I thought about Sarah, sitting next to me on the plane. She is a beautiful young woman and she has a lot to offer to anyone who takes the time to understand who she is and the strength she has. She also has a gentle touch and an appealing smile. I'm sure it was the gentle touch and smile that the little girl at the orphanage understood.

I stated before in this narrative that I'm the father of three sons. They are the best of sons, good husbands, and good fathers in their own right. My life has been enriched by their presence. They have proven time and again that they are priceless beyond measure. Still, when I observe the men and women on the trip to Kili, all younger than me, some, much younger; I see people of incredible strength and depth. They are survivors, caregivers, spouses and friends. They are, in one way or another much like Mary and Sarah;

people of rare courage and sensitivity; people who care, not just about themselves, but about those around them. When I think about this; especially about the women, I have to wonder if maybe, just maybe; that, in life; I might have been shy a daughter.

Daylight chased our plane across the Atlantic. The same sun that bejeweled the glacier atop Kili now pushed rays ahead of us. It followed us across Labrador and Georges Bay, and caught us quickly when we turned south toward Minneapolis. The land below is cold and pockmarked with patches of snow interrupted by frozen land. Tanzania is far behind me. Desert, rainforest, plateau, and rocks are all a memory. The people I've met, both on this airplane and back in Tanzania are more like pictures in my mind than as real, moving, feeling, and active people.

Cancer, illness, and age may have slowed me. Maybe I failed at climbing Kili because of these hurdles. But there is one thing that I didn't fail. I didn't fail to see people laughing. I didn't fail to see people struggle to overcome difficulty. I didn't fail to see people live as best they could in circumstances they could not control. I didn't fail to see the injustice that has captured Tanzania; and I didn't fail to understand that I am at least partly responsible for those injustices.

The challenge of a trek to Kilimanjaro provided me with more than an opportunity to meet a group of people I came to enjoy and love. It provided me with the opportunity to spend time with myself. The time in the airplane, the time in the trucks, and the time spent walking for four days up the mountain gave me a once in a lifetime adventure of visiting Africa and walking up the highest mountain on that continent. The time within myself gave me the luxury of thinking about my life with cancer and what may lie ahead for me.

I wouldn't say that the experience of diagnosis; surgery, reoccurrence, checkups, radiation, a second reoccurrence, and hormone treatment; has helped me to come closer to God. I would say that all of this, as well as the ongoing testing and treatments, have made me more aware of God. I have become more aware of God in his magnificent creation. I have become more aware of God in my day to day world and I have become more aware of God in those around me.

I see clearly the evidence of the Creator in Mount Kilimanjaro, the evidence of the Son in all the good things that people say and do for each other, and all the healing of the Spirit that we witness through the hands and minds of physicians who work in concert with Him. I also see clearly the stages of life that I have experienced, am experiencing, and will experience. In this sense, cancer has changed my life for the better, as it mocks any sense of invincibility I may have, or have had.

I don't fear death, or, the process of dying. I do fear pain, but I know that pain can, for the most part, be controlled. My oncologist tells me that eventually the cancer will figure out how to defeat the hormone treatment. Then, in terms of today's available treatment, I would receive chemotherapy. The idea is to keep putting roadblocks in front of the cancer to slow it down in the hope that I'll live to a ripe old age, barring accident or other malady. This is OK by me. It's OK because I intend to find another mountain to climb. I intend to go to another exotic place, meet people, enjoy the views and enjoy the company. I also intend to make it to the top of that mountain; wherever or whatever that may be.

Dr. Greg Higgins with a child at Orphanage.

TOP OF AFRICA

Your arms of white beckoned me.
Your majesty intrigued me.
Your mystery amazed me,
And I answered.

I answered you
To see, to hear, and to sense
All that might be within me.
And I shuddered.

I saw your pink tinge at sunrise.
I saw your bare slopes in daylight.
I saw your treed flanks in dewdrop.
I saw your barren footprints.

I heard the wind blow wild.
I heard the cries of simian and fowl.
I heard the wash of your moving waters;
Your splendor called again.

My body pushed forward,
My mind raced within,
My lungs begged for air,
And limbs ached for rest.

Rest came easy,
Rest came warm,
Rest soothed pain,
Resolve strengthened.

Strengthened for what?
Strength with a flaw,
Strength denied,
I'd given my all.

Call again, Mighty Mountain,
Call again and I'll come.
Call again, ease my sorrow,
I'll come to you, Kilimanjaro.

ACKNOWLEDGEMENTS

WRITING A BOOK doesn't come easy. It was only because of the people I met on this adventure to Tanzania and Mount Kilimanjaro that I decided to put my thoughts on paper. First of all, I want to thank all the participants, whether cancer survivors, care givers, supporters, guides, or porters for accepting me as I am. Each person on the trip contributed to my growth as a person, both physically and spiritually. I am grateful to all of them for their friendship, collegiality, and patience. You will be a part of this person I call "me," for the rest of my life.

I am especially appreciative of Dr. Richard Deming. His thoughtfulness, caring presence, and his skill as a physician-radiologist, all combined to allow me to realize a greater potential for myself as a cancer survivor. His passion for healthy living and his ability to hear the thoughts and feel the joys, sorrows, and pain of his patients and their families is unparalleled.

Charlie Wittmack is one of the most unusual men I have been privileged to meet. He is always outgoing and positive. Without his encouragement and expertise as an adventurer, the journey to Africa wouldn't have been possible. His "can do" spirit is courteous, unrelenting and contagious.

Yasmina Madden, MFA, and Visiting Professor of English at Drake University, was an invaluable coach and mentor of my writing process. Her encouragement and expert critique of my work is greatly appreciated. Professor Madden's insight was the catalyst for my decision that it would be helpful, not only for me, but for others, to write about the emotions that I had encountered over the course of twenty three years as a cancer patient.

I would like to give a special thank you to Mary VanHeukelom and Sarah Russell, both of whom gave me permission to include them as a part of this book in greater detail. Both of them provided me with a greater understanding of a younger generation, especially from the feminine point of view. An additional thank you to General Chombo and Jonathan is in order. In all likelihood, neither of these men will have an opportunity to read these words, but both men impressed on me the quality of their character and the potential of the Tanzanian nation.

Last but not least, an appreciative hug for my wife, Cora, for putting up with my spending hours in front of a computer while she went about her days with no one to talk to. An additional hug is in order for her skill as an editor, and her gift to me of accepting my decision to go to Africa in the first place.

NOTE TO THE READER

ALL PROFITS FROM the sale of this book will be donated to Above & Beyond Cancer or to the Kilimanjaro Orphanage.

Those who wish may make donations directly may send them to:

**Above and Beyond Cancer
1915 Grand Avenue
Des Mines, IA 50309**

Please note if your donation is for Above & Beyond Cancer or The Kilimanjaro Orphanage

Additional Information about Above & Beyond Cancer is available at:
Above & Beyond Cancer.org.